"If you've participated in women's Bible studies, you kn⸺⸺ on Esther written for female audiences. Why consider th⸺ ⸺⸺ full ten weeks to moving line-by-line through a mere ten chapters, employing excellent and accessible study skills along the way. But even better than that, *Esther: The Hidden Hand of God* points us beyond Esther herself to the One she served. Here is a study intent on making disciples who know and worship their God."

Jen Wilkin, Bible teacher; author, *Women of the Word*; *None Like Him*; and *In His Image*

"The brilliant and beautiful mix of sound teaching, helpful charts, lists, sidebars, and appealing graphics—as well as insightful questions that get the reader into the text of Scripture—makes this a study women will want to invest time in and will look back on as time well spent."

Nancy Guthrie, author, Seeing Jesus in the Old Testament Bible study series

"If you're looking for a rich, accessible, and deeply biblical Bible study, this is it! Lydia Brownback leads her readers verse-by-verse through Esther, providing maps, timelines, commentary, and questions that probe the text in order to glean understanding and application. She settles us deeply in the context of the book as she highlights God's unfolding plan of redemption and rescue. You will learn, you will delight in God's word, and you will love our good King Jesus even more."

Courtney Doctor, Coordinator of Women's Initiatives, The Gospel Coalition; author, *From Garden to Glory* and *Steadfast: A Devotional Bible Study on the Book of James*

"*Esther: The Hidden Hand of God* provides a visually engaging study with accessible content to help women understand the content of the book of Esther in the context of the whole counsel of Scripture. As a women's ministry leader, I am excited about the development of the Flourish Bible Study series that will not only prayerfully equip women to increase in biblical literacy but also come alongside them to build a systematic and comprehensive framework to become lifelong students of the word of God."

Karen Hodge, Women's Ministry Coordinator, Presbyterian Church in America

"Lydia Brownback's Bible study on Esther is a sturdy and faithful guide for us. Providing rich insights into context, guiding our investigation into details of the text, and encouraging us to respond to the character and work of the unmentioned God, it helps us better know our Bible and our saving and sovereign Lord. I will recommend it for years to come for those looking for a wise, Christ-centered study that leads toward the goal of being transformed by the word."

Taylor Turkington, Director of Women's Training Network, The Gospel Coalition

ESTHER

Flourish Bible Study Series
by Lydia Brownback

Esther: The Hidden Hand of God

FLOURISH
BIBLE STUDY

ESTHER

THE HIDDEN HAND OF GOD

LYDIA BROWNBACK

CROSSWAY®

WHEATON, ILLINOIS

Crossway is a publishing ministry of Good News Publishers.

RRDS		29	28	27	26	25	24	23	22	21	20
15	14	13	12	11	10	9	8	7	6	5	4	3	2	1

With gratitude to God
for
Paula Wilding,
a dear friend who courageously, boldly,
and consistently stands for truth

CONTENTS

THE PLACE OF ESTHER
IN BIBLICAL HISTORY

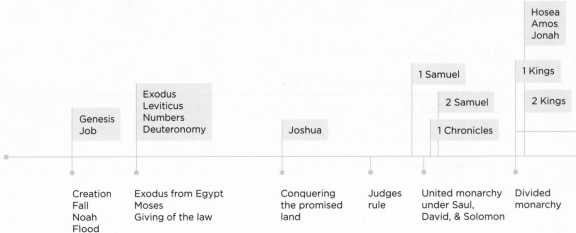

Hosea
Amos
Jonah

1 Samuel

1 Kings

Exodus
Leviticus
Numbers
Deuteronomy

2 Samuel

2 Kings

Genesis
Job

Joshua

1 Chronicles

Creation
Fall
Noah
Flood
Abraham

Exodus from Egypt
Moses
Giving of the law

Conquering
the promised
land

Judges
rule

United monarchy
under Saul,
David, & Solomon

Divided
monarchy

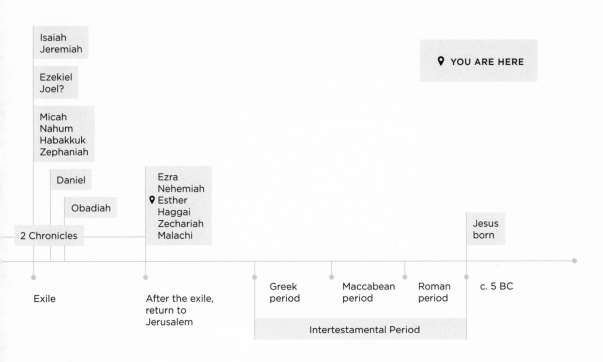

YOU ARE HERE

Isaiah
Jeremiah

Ezekiel
Joel?

Micah
Nahum
Habakkuk
Zephaniah

Daniel

Obadiah

Ezra
Nehemiah
Esther
Haggai
Zechariah
Malachi

Jesus
born

2 Chronicles

Exile

After the exile,
return to
Jerusalem

Greek
period

Maccabean
period

Roman
period

c. 5 BC

Intertestamental Period

INTRODUCTION

Once upon a time . . . that's how all good fairy tales begin, and it's a good way to begin our study of Esther. But Esther is no fairy tale. This book of the Bible records very real events in a very real time in the history of God's people. Over the centuries there have been people—even influential church people like Martin Luther—who believe that the book of Esther is a fairy tale. They believe that Esther shouldn't be included as one of the books of the Bible, primarily because God isn't mentioned in the book.

That *is* kind of amazing, isn't it? The Bible—the written revelation of God himself—contains a book that has no mention of God at all. But we'll see that he really is there in Esther—he's just hidden. The fact that God isn't mentioned in this book is actually purposeful, and it points out something vitally important about him and his ways. Most of all, we're going to see how the book of Esther points us to our Lord and Savior Jesus Christ. He isn't mentioned in the book either, but he is most definitely there!

CHARACTERS

God is the main figure of our story, of course, even though he is hidden. And then the anonymous author of this Bible book shows us an intriguing cast of characters, including Esther herself. She is a young Jewish orphan girl being raised by her older cousin Mordecai in ancient Persia. Mordecai also plays an important role in the story, as we shall see. Then there's Haman, a rising government official in Persia. He is the primary villain of our story. Haman serves King Ahasuerus (also known as King Xerxes), and this king figures prominently in the story as well. We encounter Queen Vashti, although she disappears from the story early on. And there are a few other minor characters serving in the king's court. When we consider the characters of the story, we must also include all the Jews—God's very own people—who were living in Persia at this time.

Pronunciation Guide

Agagite: AH-ga-gite

Ahasuerus: a-HASS-u-air-es

Esther: EST-er

Harbona: har-BONE-a

Hadassah: ha-DASS-a

Haman: HAY-man

Hathach: HAY-thack

Hegai: HAY-guy

Memucan: mem-U-can

Mordecai: MOR-de-kie

pur: poor

Purim: POOR-em

Vashti: VASH-tie

Zeresh: ZEER-esh

SETTING

Here at the outset of our study, it's important to say something about the setting of the story. The events recorded in Esther take place primarily in the city of Susa, a thriving hub of Persia where the king spent the winter months. These events occurred over the course of a decade in the fifth century BC, when King Ahasuerus ruled a vast empire, the Persian Empire, which included almost all of the Middle East.

Many years before our story takes place—long before Persia became the world superpower—God's people had lived securely in the land God had given them, Canaan, the "promised land." But after taking possession of the land, they grew careless toward God and turned away from him to worship other gods—false gods. For a long, long time, they refused to repent of their sin, so they fell under God's judgment. Their punishment was exile from the comfort and security of the promised land. They were taken captive by the Babylonians, forced to leave their homeland, and made to live in pagan Babylon. There they remained for many decades. This period of time in Israelite history is called "the exile." It was a heartbreaking time, but it was heartbreak that God's people had brought on themselves by their determined and ongoing refusal to repent of spiritual adultery, of unfaithfulness to the Lord. You might want to take a few minutes to read Psalm 137, which gives us a glimpse of the heartache they experienced during the exile. Sometimes—both then and now—God disciplines his people in painful ways to draw wayward hearts back to him.

Timeline	
722 BC–586 BC	God's people are forced to leave the promised land and carried away captive to Babylon.
539 BC	King Cyrus of Persia conquers the Babylonian Empire and sets up a new kingdom that gives freedom to God's people.
538 BC–445 BC	God's people return to their homeland. The story of Esther takes place in this time frame, from 483 to 473 BC.

Over time, however, the powerful Babylonian Empire grew weak and was eventually conquered by the rising power of Persia under King Cyrus.

When King Cyrus took over Babylon, he allowed God's people, the Jews, to return to their homeland. He even provided government aid so they could rebuild all that had been destroyed when the Babylonians had invaded. The Persian king's generosity toward God's people was most likely just shrewd political strategy. Happy subjects would surely be loyal subjects, willing to fork over their money for Persian taxes.

King Cyrus may have used the Jews for his own purposes, but what really matters is that God was using King Cyrus. In fact, King Cyrus came to power solely because God raised him up. We know this from the prophet Isaiah. Before the exile had even taken place, God spoke through Isaiah, declaring that he would use Cyrus, this future foreign king, to deliver his people and bring them home from exile:

> Thus says the LORD to his anointed, to Cyrus,
>   whose right hand I have grasped,
> to subdue nations before him
>   and to loose the belts of kings,
> to open doors before him
>   that gates may not be closed:
> "I will go before you
>   and level the exalted places,

I will break in pieces the doors of bronze
    and cut through the bars of iron,
I will give you the treasures of darkness
    and the hoards in secret places,
that you may know that it is I, the LORD,
    the God of Israel, who call you by your name.
For the sake of my servant Jacob,
    and Israel my chosen,
I call you by your name,
    I name you, though you do not know me.
I am the LORD, and there is no other,
    besides me there is no God;
    I equip you, though you do not know me,
that people may know, from the rising of the sun
    and from the west, that there is none besides me;
    I am the LORD, and there is no other.
I form light and create darkness;
    I make well-being and create calamity;
    I am the LORD, who does all these things." (Isaiah 45:1–7)

God worked his will through Cyrus, this foreign king, which demonstrates that every human being—great or small, strong or weak—is under God's authority. This even includes people who don't believe in God.

What does all this have to do with the book of Esther? Well, the king of our story, King Ahasuerus, was Cyrus's grandson. And the fact that two generations have passed since God's people, the Jews, were allowed to return to Israel makes us wonder why many had not gone home but had chosen to remain in Persia. Perhaps so many of God's people stayed because, over time, they had adapted to the culture of Persia. They'd grown so comfortable that a significant number no longer cared about returning home to Jerusalem, the heart of the promised land.

Years before, when the exiled Jews had been forced to come to this foreign land, no doubt they experienced significant culture shock, but God had provided them with instructions for how to survive it. Through the prophet Jeremiah, God encouraged his people to persevere:

> Thus says the LORD of hosts, the God of Israel, to all the exiles whom I have sent into exile from Jerusalem to Babylon: Build houses and live in them; plant gardens and eat their produce. Take wives and have sons and daughters; take wives for your sons, and give your daughters in marriage, that they may bear sons and daughters; multiply there, and do not decrease. But seek the welfare of the city where I have sent you into exile, and pray to the LORD on its behalf, for in its welfare you will find your welfare. (Jeremiah 29:4–7)

God's people had heeded those instructions and settled down. But God had never intended them to settle *permanently* in Babylon:

> For thus says the LORD: When seventy years are completed for Babylon, I will visit you, and I will fulfill to you my promise and bring you back to this place. For I know the plans I have for you, declares the LORD, plans for welfare and not for evil, to give you a future and a hope. Then you will call upon me and come and pray to me, and I will hear you. You will seek me and find me, when you seek me with all your heart. I will be found by you, declares the LORD, and I will restore your fortunes and gather you from all the nations and all the places where I have driven you, declares the LORD, and I will bring you back to the place from which I sent you into exile. (Jeremiah 29:10–14)

As that first exiled generation died out, some of God's people lost sight of Jeremiah's words. Once they'd settled into Babylonian life, they developed a taste for its luxuries, and over time their longing for home likely diminished. They grew content to live dispersed throughout the Middle East under these pagan governing authorities. A large number of them forgot the Lord—his covenant and his promises—so by the time of Esther, they were contented with Persian life, whether in the city of Susa or in one of the many outlying provinces governed by the Persian king.

We face similar temptations today, don't we? It's easy to settle into the comforts of our culture, all the freedoms and luxuries available to us. Yet as we enjoy them, we can come to depend on them for our well-being, and then God and his ways get pushed into the background of our hearts. We want to be on guard against this, and it's something we can pray for here at the beginning of our study.

PLOT AND THEMES

We will uncover the plot of Esther as we make our way through the study, but we can set out the big picture here. The book of Esther recounts how a secret plan to exterminate God's people, the Jews, gets set in motion but is overturned by God in surprising ways. That is the plot, and through it we can identify the overarching theme of Esther: *God is faithful to keep his promises and to deliver his people.*

There are other themes in Esther that we will uncover as we proceed. The *providence of God* is a theme that's threaded all through the book, and we will look closely at that. Another intriguing theme is *reversal*, the way in which God turns things around. We will see why he is sometimes referred to as "the God of reversals." As we make our way through the book, we will also notice how often scenes are built around feasts or banquets. And while we are on the subject, it's good to note right here that the story of Esther was originally written to record the origin of an important Jewish celebration—the Feast of Purim—which is still celebrated annually today, usually in the month of March. (We'll discuss Purim more in week 10).

Above all, we want to uncover how *the story of Esther points to Jesus Christ and his gospel.* Here's a glimpse: our story exposes the need for a better deliverer, a better king, and a better kingdom than any we find in this world. This is the primary consideration to set before us as we study God's word together.

> *Our story exposes the need for a better deliverer, a better king, and a better kingdom than any we find in this world.*

STUDYING ESTHER

At the beginning of each week's lesson, read the entire passage. And then read it again. If you are studying Esther with a group, read it once more, aloud, when you gather to discuss the lesson. *Marinating in the Scripture text is the most important aspect of any Bible study.*

GROUP STUDY

If you are doing this study as part of a group, you'll want to finish each week's lesson before the group meeting. You can work your way through the study questions all in one sitting or by doing a little bit each day. And don't be discouraged if you don't have time to answer every question. Just do as much as you can, knowing that the more you do, the more you'll learn. No matter how much of the study you are able to complete each week, the group will benefit just from having you there, so don't skip if you can't finish! That being said, group time will be most rewarding for every participant if you have done the lesson in advance.

If you are leading the group, you can download the free leader's guide at https://www.flourish/esther/leadersguide.

INDIVIDUAL STUDY

The study is designed to run for ten weeks, but you can set your own pace if you're studying solo. And you can also download the free leader's guide (https://www.flourish/esther/leadersguide) if you'd like some guidance along the way.

Reading Plan

	Primary Text	Supplemental Reading
Week 1	Esther 1:1–22	Exodus 17:8–16; 1 Samuel 15:1–33
Week 2	Esther 2:1–23	
Week 3	Esther 3:1–15	
Week 4	Esther 4:1–17	Genesis 12:1–3; 2 Samuel 7:8–16; Isaiah 43:1–7
Week 5	Esther 5:1–14	
Week 6	Esther 6:1–14	
Week 7	Esther 7:1–10	
Week 8	Esther 8:1–17	
Week 9	Esther 9:1–19	Isaiah 32:1–8; Revelation 19:6–9
Week 10	Esther 9:20–10:3	

A KING'S FEAST

ESTHER 1:1-22

Dinner parties were a big, lavish deal in ancient Persia. As we will see, there are several such parties—big feasts—in Esther (see the "Feasts in Esther" chart on p. 22), and each one leads to a turning point in the story. We find three parties in the first chapter of Esther alone! The first party (vv. 1–4) was hosted by the king for his official cabinet and VIPs from around the Persian kingdom. Since the party lasted for 180 days—that's six months!—it's best to understand it as a series of civic festivities over this period, interspersed with magnificent feasts. This months-long celebration came after endless rounds of military meetings in which plans were made to stand up against Greece, a rising power on the world stage.

When the six months of pomp and ceremony were done, King Ahasuerus threw another party for the locals who had worked hard to make Susa nice for the VIP events. While this weeklong party for the locals was going on, the king's wife, Queen Vashti, hosted her own party for the local women.

Lavishness of all kinds abounded at Persian dinner parties, and drink was as important as food. Wine connoisseurs in those days were a lot like members of today's wine clubs, where enthusiasts gather to share their knowledge and sample various vintages. In Persia, even the vessels for wine were significant and often made of pure gold.

Feasts in Esther	
Esther 1:3–4	King Ahasuerus hosts a celebration for Persian officials.
Esther 1:5–8	King Ahasuerus hosts a feast for citizens of Susa.
Esther 1:9	Queen Vashti hosts a feast for the women of Susa.
Esther 2:18	King Ahasuerus hosts a feast in honor of his new queen, Esther.
Esther 3:15	King Ahasuerus and Haman drink to celebrate the edict against the Jews.
Esther 5:4–8	Esther prepares a feast for King Ahasuerus and Haman.
Esther 5:12–14; 6:14–7:1	Esther prepares a second feast for King Ahasuerus and Haman.
Esther 8:17	The Jews celebrate deliverance from Haman's plot.
Esther 9:17–22	The Jews establish an annual feast to celebrate the annihilation of their enemies.

1. PORTRAIT OF A KING

We get a pretty good look at King Ahasuerus in this first chapter, and the picture the author paints gives us some insight into the king's character.

✦ What is revealed about the king in the following verses?

· verses 3–4

Heb. brown noan

multi-million $ feast of wine · He has extravagant wealth. note: Motive — he is about to launch a milita campaign to capture Greece and make himself supreme ruler of the world. He wants their support.

— He is making it obvious that he has the financial resources to support the campaign

· verses 7–8

extravagant & riches, wealth
no self-control

· verses 10–11

low regard for his wife - he just considers her
another of his material possessions to display

· verse 12   rage, anger burned within him

He had the expectation that he could have her do
whatever he wanted even if was degrading and
insulting to her dignity

· verses 19–21

✤ Summarize how King Ahasuerus is portrayed. Try to describe him in a sentence
or two.

a proud, arrogant, chauvenistic pig egotistical
sarcastic

The Persian Empire at the Time of Esther[1]

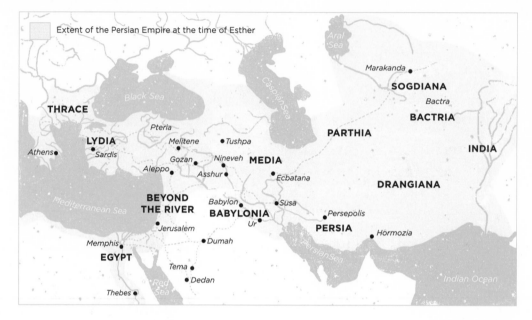

2. FEASTS FIT FOR A KING (1:3-8)

The author of Esther gives lots of details about the setting of King Ahasuerus's second banquet, the seven-day feast for the locals in Susa (see vv. 5–7). As guests entered the court of the garden of the king's palace and found their places at the banqueting table, we can imagine that they felt grateful to their host, the king, and talked among themselves about his lavish bounty. Best of all, each guest was allowed to eat and drink whatever he wanted. At most royal Persian feasts, guests were required to eat and drink whatever was set before them. Just think about that for a minute. No one could say a polite "No, thank you" to a slice of roasted goat or a dish of eggplant stew, nor could guests refrain from wine and other alcoholic drinks. But at this particular banquet, the one for the locals, the king allowed his guests to pick and choose what to consume (v. 8).

From what we've observed about King Ahasuerus so far, what might have motivated him to be so generous toward his subjects and to bend this banqueting rule?

He wanted their support. He was buttering them up

---

3. NO PLACE FOR A QUEEN (1:10-12)

On the final day of King Ahasuerus's feast, he commanded the eunuchs who served him to get Queen Vashti and bring her to his party. She was apparently very beautiful, and the king wanted to show her off to his guests. But Queen Vashti refused to come.

We aren't told why she refused, but ancient customs give us an idea. Queens and head wives attended these lavish banquets alongside their host husbands, but after the wine had flowed and the guests had become drunk and rowdy, wives left the party and were replaced by concubines—women of less social stature whose calling was solely to entertain the king through music, dance, and sexual favors (we will learn more about these concubines in week 2). Here at King Ahasuerus's party, we know that the king and his guests were drunk, so, given the timing, it could be that Queen Vashti refused to obey the king's order because she objected to being treated as a concubine. Whatever her reason, she refused the king.

Eunuchs

Eunuchs were castrated males who served in the Persian court. They had virtually no sexual capabilities, so they were considered trustworthy to serve in the harems, protecting the concubines and providing for their needs. Court eunuchs could rise to prominent positions, some even serving as trusted advisors to the king.

✦ The author tells us that the king summoned Queen Vashti when his heart "was merry with wine" (v. 10). How do the following passages from the Bible's wisdom literature help us understand from this detail something more about King Ahasuerus's character?

· Proverbs 31:4–5

He was not wise and had a low regard for others

· Ecclesiastes 10:17

He was a lousy leader

✦ Based on what we've seen of King Ahasuerus thus far, why do you think Vashti's refusal enraged him?

it was a public display of She embarrassed him and made him look foolish to his subjects

4. THE KING'S DILEMMA (1:13–21)

Queen Vashti's refusal to come to the party is a public relations nightmare for the king. No one is allowed to refuse his orders, and now his very own queen has done it! So King Ahasuerus asks his wise men for advice about how to handle the situation. These wise men were the king's advisors. They functioned in his court very much like the cabinet of the US President, offering guidance on military strategy and affairs of state. The particular wise men here are named (v. 14). These seven men made up the king's inner circle, and each of the seven were princes in various regions of the kingdom.

✦ We are told in verse 14 that the wise men were seated beside the king so that they "saw the king's face." What does this indicate about what guided the wise men as they advised the king?

> they say what they think he wants to hear

✦ One of these wise men was named Memucan. What concerns does he express in verses 16–18 and what claim does he make? Why do you think his claim would have a powerful impact on the king?

> When all the other wives hear of Vashti's behavior, being a leader and example, they will follow.

✦ Memucan suggests that the king issue a royal order barring Queen Vashti from the king's presence for all time (v. 19). Such orders, once recorded in Persian law books, could never be repealed. Memucan's suggestion pleases King Ahasuerus, and he issues the order, commanding that the decree be published far and wide throughout his vast kingdom. What anticipated response to the decree pleased the king and the princes (vv. 20–21)?

> Proper respect & subordination

5. HAIL TO THE KING!

Our story so far has all the makings of a mass-market paperback—royalty, political intrigue, unrestrained hedonism, and a very public marital breakup. Front and center is King Ahasuerus. Thoughtful study reveals him to be a rather self-centered, power-hungry, and insecure ruler. And although he delights his guests with lavish food and wine, we can guess that his motives are less about blessing his subjects than about securing their loyalty and glorifying his own name.

Think for a minute about the Jews living in Susa at this time who would have attended the feast. No doubt all these Persian luxuries did nothing to stir up desire to return to their homeland. Yet surely among them were some who could detect the seriously flawed character of this king who ruled over them, and perhaps this reality awakened in their hearts a longing for home and for what life had been like under kings who loved the Lord God. Then again, those former kings had grown increasingly wicked over time, which is why God's people came under the rule of King Ahasuerus in the first place. Yes, the glory days of Israel were long gone, just as the prophets had warned, but with those warnings the prophets had also proclaimed God's promise—the best king of all was yet to come.

✦ How is this promised king a stark contrast to King Ahasuerus?

· Isaiah 32:1–8 *Wise* ... *Fool* *They will change → not be the same after being in his presence*

streams of water in a dry land — shade for the parched and weary — Rules of righteousness the promised KING will reign in righteousness so will His princes — They will be a hiding place from the wind and shelter from a storm nobleness will be honored, subjects will respond correctly

· Jeremiah 23:5–6

He will reign and act wisely, He will do those things that accomplish justice and righteousness in the land. Judah will be saved Israel will dwell safely

The LORD is our righteousness

· Zechariah 9:9

He is righteous + endowed with salvation, Humble and submissive to the will of the Father. (riding on a donkey)

❖ Read Psalm 2, a song God's people sang back home in Israel. What is promised in this psalm? How might this psalm have helped the Jews living under Persian rule?

Promise of Holy King, Hope of God's rescue

6. THE VERY BEST BANQUET

Esther isn't the only place in Scripture where lavish feasts are on display. We find them also as invitations to God's kingdom. *Feasts as invitations to God's Kingdom*

❖ What do you see in the invitations below that make them so superior to the feasts of King Ahasuerus?

· Proverbs 9:1–6 *Wisdom is the Person inviting and preparing the banquet*

- Everyone is invited
the simple + unwise are invited

· Isaiah 55:1–3

Everyone is invited, those who cannot pay the only motive of this invitation is LOVE and life

· John 7:37–38

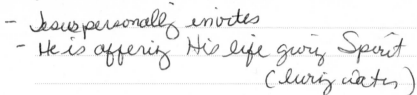

- Jesus personally invites
- He is offering His life giving Spirit
  (living water)

✦ Ultimately, all the banquet invitations in the Bible point to the ultimate invitation—the marriage supper of the Lamb—which is the be-all-end-all feast that believers will one day eat with the Lord in glory. What can we look forward to there?

· Isaiah 25:6–9

- a wonderful feast of well-aged wine and choice meat
- a delicious banquet

· Revelation 19:7–9

Wedding feast of the LAMB
clothed in righteous deeds

LET'S TALK

1. You might be wondering what our focus on kingship this week has to do with real life—with *your* life. But who rules you is actually the most important thing about your life. We all bow down to something or someone. If it isn't King Jesus, it's money or beauty or pleasure of the sort on display in Persia. There's no getting around it: if we're not worshiping King Jesus, we are worshiping something or someone else, and whatever it might be, it's actually nothing more than a tyrant like King Ahasuerus masquerading as a generous host. Can you identify anyone or anything in your life that pushes the Lord away? Is there something or someone that tempts you to say, "I will not have this king—King Jesus—to rule

over me" (see Luke 19:14)? If so, identify a practical step you can take this very week to help you change.

Serving as an act of worship those who really irritate me. 😊

2. Kingship in the Bible isn't just about actual kings. It's ultimately about *authority*. We all live under the authority of others in every sphere of life. As citizens, we are subject to the government. As church members, we are subject to the oversight of pastors and elders. Employees are under the authority of bosses, and wives are called to submit to the loving leadership of their husbands. In what area of life is submission a struggle for you, and why? How does knowing Jesus as your King of kings help you with this struggle?

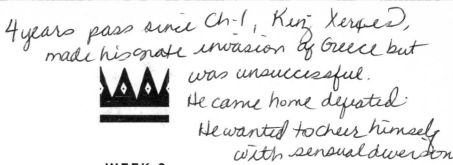

4 years pass since Ch-1, King Xerxes, made his great invasion of Greece but was unsuccessful. He came home defeated. He wanted to cheer himself with sensual diversion

AN UNLIKELY QUEEN

ESTHER 2:1-23

God controls everything. All the time. We might not be able to see his hand at work in our circumstances, but we can be sure he is directing our course in every detail. Even more, he is directing the course of the whole world and working in everything and everyone to the ends he intends. That is exactly what we are supposed to get from the unfolding of events in Esther 2. God has a plan, and he is slowly and surely working it out in Persia.

Divine providence—his guiding rule—is at work in high places. It's active in the king's court and even in the king's emotions. God is also at work in ordinary Persian households and on the city streets of Susa. Although God isn't mentioned even once in the story, he is working through the hearts of leaders, through the beautiful features of young women, and through calculating servants. In all the ordinary details of ordinary Persian life, God is bringing about his purposes.

1. A KING WITHOUT A QUEEN (2:1-4)

Insecurity and anger make for a lethal combination, which we saw clearly from King Ahasuerus in week 1. Queen Vashti's refusal to respond to the king's summons had not only enraged the king; it had humiliated him too. So in the heat of anger and in an attempt to soothe his wounded ego, he had banished the queen forever. Over time, however, the king's unruly emotions calmed, and his perspective changed.

We're told that King Ahasuerus "remembered Vashti and what she had done and what had been decreed against her" (v. 1). Based on the guidance supplied by the young advisors in verse 2, what sort of "remembering" was the king most likely doing?

sensual desiring

Identify each of the four steps suggested by the advisors in verses 2–4.

1. *search be conducted on the king's behalf for* *attractive women*
2. *appoint officers to gather all attractive women* *to Susa citadel harem* *(under Hegai)*
3. *let the king's enuchs oversee them and provide cosmetics* *beauty treatments*
4. *let the one the king finds most attractive be made queen in place of Vashti*

We have considered the unfolding events from the king's perspective, but let's think now about the young women of Persia. The first part of the administration's plan was a search—an organized search for a new queen—and the primary qualification for a new queen was physical beauty. Once candidates were identified, these young beauties were taken out of their homes and brought to the harem in Susa, where they would live under the authority of the chief eunuch, Hegai. The young women had no say in the matter, and most likely their parents or guardians didn't either. These beauties were forced to forgo whatever hopes and dreams they might have had for their lives. Even so, no doubt some of the young women delighted to be among those chosen, because it provided them an opportunity to become the next queen. For all but one of the young women, however, any anticipation would be short-lived.

2. MORDECAI AND ESTHER (2:5-11)

In this section we meet Mordecai. He is a Jew, one of God's people. Mordecai's great-grandfather was among those carried away captive when Jerusalem fell to King Nebuchadnezzar of Babylon. (For a brief refresher, refer back to page 14). Now, three generations later, here is Mordecai, an Israelite from an elite family, living in Persia. He is raising a young female cousin named Hadassah, but this young Jewish girl is better known by her Persian name, Esther, which means "star." More important than the meaning of her Persian name is what that name represents—that her outward identity at this point is perhaps more Persian than Jewish.

Because of Esther's beauty, she was among the young women who were gathered up and taken to the king's harem, where she was treated better than many of the young women. Why, according to verse 9, was she treated so well?

"She was good in his eyes"
he was very impressed w/ her.
She found favor in his sight.

Mordecai

Mordecai descended from the tribe of Benjamin (Esther 2:5). The first book of the Bible, Genesis, includes the story of Jacob and his twelve sons, one of which was Benjamin. The descendants of these twelve sons became the twelve tribes of Israel.

✦ Why did Esther hold back her Jewish identity? What does this secrecy likely indicate about the place of God's people, the Jews, in Persian society at the time?

Mordecai instructed her not to disclose her identity

3. THE REALITY OF HAREM LIFE (2:12-14)

Mordecai is concerned for his young ward, so he paces outside the harem each day in hopes of learning how Esther is faring. He needn't have worried. Behind closed doors, Esther is participating in a twelve-month beauty ritual. Many readers of Esther like to pause here and imagine how great that must have been. And in some ways it probably was, but we are likely to change our thinking when we understand a bit more about this beauty ritual and the realities of harem life.

First, we need to cast aside the idea that life in the harem was a delightfully endless spa package with all the trimmings. Sure, there were lovely fragrances and soft music and luxurious treatments, but women in the harem also faced danger and dislike. That's because each woman was competing with all the other women for the king's favor, and each had only one chance to capture it—a single night alone with the king.

Women of the Persian Harem[2]

- Received an education
- Learned horsemanship and archery
- Participated in hunting expeditions
- Traveled and attended feasts
- Managed servants and professional laborers
- Acquired wealth

On the designated night, each young woman "was given whatever she desired to take with her from the harem" (v. 13). Most likely, she took along special clothes and various tools of seduction. We don't need to sugarcoat what was going on here, because the Bible certainly doesn't. These nights were solely about pleasing the king, attempting to intrigue him and spark his affections with every sensual trick of the trade.

After sharing the king's bed all night, a young woman was sent to a different section of the harem, the so-called second harem. If her one night with the king was a failure—if she failed to delight him—she would remain hidden away in this second harem, out of the king's sight, for the rest of her life. In light of all this, no doubt the harem was characterized by fierce—and sometimes vicious—competition.

As for those beauty treatments that sound so great, well, perhaps they were. We are told that each woman underwent six months of beautifying with oil of myrrh and then six months with spices and ointments. We picture how great our skin would look after that, right? But we have to realize that we live with scientific advantages that women in that day did not. The young women of Persia went into the harem in an age with limited knowledge of germs and bacteria and medical conditions. So, very likely, at least some of these skin treatments were applied as remedies for fungal infections and other unpleasant bodily ailments that could have been a turnoff to the king or, worst-case scenario, infected him.

✦ Esther won Hegai's favor and was rewarded with personal attendants, tasty food, and superior accommodations, and her days were spent luxuriating in baths and learning the arts of seduction—all while keeping her Jewish identity a secret. The author passes no judgment on Esther or her life within the harem. In fact, as we will see, the author never addresses the morality of anything Esther does. How can this serve as a guide to our own thinking about Esther?

She was probably meek & lowly, the hidden she was not a harlot, she would, with the other concubines, become his wife (secondary)

4. ESTHER'S NIGHT (2:15–17)

The time finally comes for Esther's night alone with King Ahasuerus, a night for which she has been preparing for many months. Her efforts are rewarded, for the king finds her fascinating. In fact, we are told that he loves her. Remembrances of the former Queen Vashti are driven from his mind, and he promptly sets a crown on Esther's head, making her his new queen.

We are told that Esther, while in the harem, "was winning favor" in the eyes of all who saw her (v. 15) and later that she "won grace and favor" in the king's sight. The favor shown Esther was something she *won*. Based on what we've seen of Esther so far, how did she go about winning favor? (You might want to take another look at verses 10 and 15.)

Esther was discreet, she was respectful and submissive to Mordecai's authority, not outward and greedy

In celebration of his new queen, Ahasuerus throws another feast—the fourth one in the story—and keeping with tradition at celebratory occasions, he also gives Persian citizens a tax break and lavishes gifts on his subjects.

As you consider how the story has unfolded so far, how can you trace God's hand at work behind the scenes, guiding the steps of Esther's life? Note where you can discern the hand of God working through

- King Ahasuerus (1:5, 10–12, 21–22; 2:1, 4, 16–18):

The feast led him to be "merry" drunkenness led him to want to sexually exploit Vashti, her rejection led to him being without a queen, his loneliness led him to want Vashti back or another queen

· Queen Vashti (1:12, 19):

her refusal caused her to be dethroned and the
king was left without a prize queen

· The king's young advisors (2:2–4):

seeing the king's loneliness and desire made a way for
the advisors to devise a plan for the king to
pick a new queen

· Hegai the eunuch (2:8–9, 15):

He providentially was in charge of the young virgins,
Esther found favor in his sight, so she got all
the best and the extras, she was respectful and submissive
to Hegai's authority "he advised"

· Mordecai (2:5–7, 10–11):

Mordecai providentially became Esther's guardian.
Mordecai had given Esther wise counsel and she listened.
v19 Mordecai was providentially had a job of "sitting
at the king's gate" — he was there to hear the evil plans
against the king"

✙ How do Proverbs 16:1, 9 and 21:1 reinforce your understanding of God's work in
this story?

Prov. 16:1
" The plans & reflections of the heart belong to man, but
the wise answer of the tongue is from the LORD"
v.9 " A man's mind plans his way as he journeys through
life, but the LORD directs his steps"
" The king's heart is like a channel of water in the
Prov   hand of the LORD; HE turns it whichever way HE
21:1   wishes"

5. IN THE RIGHT PLACE AT THE RIGHT TIME (2:19-23)

In this final section of Esther 2, the scene swings from Mordecai to Esther and back to Mordecai again, as a plot to kill King Ahasuerus is exposed.

✤ The scene opens on Mordecai, who is sitting in the king's gate. We mustn't think he was people watching from the comfort of a lounge chair; he was, in fact, quite busy. Gate sitters in those days were the movers and shakers and decision makers. They solved community problems and decided civil matters and legal cases. What does Mordecai's position at the gate indicate about his place in Persian society?

He was a trusted leader

✤ What do we learn about Esther—now Queen Esther—in verse 20? What does this convey about Mordecai's place in her life, even though she is now King Ahasuerus's queen?

a place of honor & respect

✤ How did the plot against the king originate?

they became angry

✦ Where do you see the providential hand of God at work in this scene of political intrigue (vv. 19–23)? Consider the various people and the events they set in motion.

_____

_____

_____

_____

_____

LET'S TALK

1. As we consider the reality of harem life in ancient Persia, we can't help but get a fresh appreciation for the freedoms we women have today. What particular freedoms do we tend to take for granted?

_____

_____

_____

_____

_____

_____

_____

2. At Mordecai's urging, Esther hid her Jewish identity from everyone in the harem and in the king's court. Do you ever hide your Christian identity? If so, in what contexts? What are you afraid of?

3. Esther won people's favor, first within the harem and then with the king. Whose favor do you seek and why? How do you attempt to win it?

AN EVIL MAN AND AN EVIL PLAN

ESTHER 3:1–15

Into the story, seemingly out of nowhere, comes a man named Haman. King Ahasuerus favored Haman, which made him a rising star in the king's administration, and before long, Haman had become a very powerful figure in Persia. In fact, at the king's decree, everyone in Persia was required to bow down to Haman and treat him like royalty. From what we know, the authority given to Haman was acceptable to Persian citizens; after all, what the king wanted, the king got, and giving honor to yet one more official was no big deal. But for Mordecai it *was* a big deal. Mordecai refused to bow to Haman, a refusal that ignited a life-or-death crisis for God's people.

1. A LOOK BACK (3:1-2)

"After these things"—the opening words of Esther 3 give us a clue about why the king put so much trust in Haman so quickly. Surely King Ahasuerus had been shaken up by the plot against him, planned by men he'd thought he could trust. After this betrayal, who could the king trust? Haman was always there soothing the king's ego and saying all the right things, so he seemed to be a good choice.

We aren't told for sure why King Ahasuerus put so much trust in Haman, but we are told that Haman was an Agagite, which indicates that he descended from a long-ago Amalekite king named Agag, who had tried to destroy God's people. The author of Esther wants us to pick up on this detail—Haman comes from a long line of a Jewish-hating people called the Amalekites.

Read Exodus 17:8–16, which describes a time when the Amalekites tried to destroy God's people. What does God decree concerning the Amalekites in Exodus 17:14–16?

GOD would blot out the amelekits

God fulfills some of his decrees slowly, over time, and this explains why the Amalekites were still on the scene and stirring up trouble centuries later during the days of Israel's first king, Saul. To deal with these troublemakers, the Lord commanded Saul to carry out that long-ago decree from back in Exodus. Saul was to destroy the Amalekites, which included Haman's infamous ancestor King Agag. Read 1 Samuel 15:1–33. How did King Saul fail to carry out the Lord's command? What ultimately happened to King Agag?

He was cut in pieces by Samuel before the LORD in Gilgal

Amalek fights Israel, and the Lord determines to blot out Amalek and his people (Exodus 17:8–16).

↓

The Lord commands King Saul to destroy the Amalekite King Agag and all the Amalekites, but Saul disobeys the Lord's command (1 Samuel 15:1–34).

↓

Haman, a descendant of King Agag, rises in the political ranks of the Persian Empire (Esther 3:1).

2. PRIDE AND PREJUDICE (3:3-6)

The backstory from Exodus and 1 Samuel gives us hints as to why Mordecai refuses to honor Haman despite the urging of the king's servants who sat alongside him at the city gate. We aren't told why Mordecai refuses to bow to Haman, but the animosity that had gone on between Israelites and Amalekites for generations is a likely reason. And this long-held tension would explain why Mordecai finally reveals to his fellow gate sitters that he is a Jew (v. 4). No doubt his gate-sitting colleagues were mystified by his animosity toward Haman and pressed him for an explanation.

🔸 How does Haman initially react when he finds out that Mordecai refuses to honor him? Where else in this story have we seen a similar reaction? Can you identify similarities in these instances as to what provoked this particular emotion?

Haman & King Xerxes were both proud arrogant & insecure. They both were filled with wrath when what they wanted did not happen.

🔸 How does verse 6 show the full extent of Haman's hatred? To whom does it extend?

all the Jews he hated

This isn't the first time—nor will it be the last—that evil plots have been hatched against God's people. The first plot happened way back in the garden of Eden, instigated by the evil serpent, and they've been happening ever since. Will evil win? Sometimes it sure looks that way. Evil seems to triumph while God seems far off and hidden. But God is always present, and he always has a plan.

3. IT'S ALL IN THE TIMING (3:7-11)

We are given some strange dates and data at the beginning of this section (v. 7), but it's really much simpler than it looks. Basically, we are meant to see that Haman is biding his time, waiting for the right opportunity to set his evil plot in motion. For guidance about the best time to strike, Haman turns to a mystical practice—casting lots—which was basically like rolling dice. The lot (called *pur*, or the plural *purim*) was cast during Nisan, the first month of the Jewish calendar, and as the process unfolds, the lot indicates that the twelfth month, Adar, would be the ideal time to kill the Jews. So, Haman has eleven months to wait before he can implement his evil intention. Even so, he takes some immediate steps.

Haman begins with an appeal to King Ahasuerus (vv. 8–9). How does he portray God's people, the Jews, in his appeal?

> They keep themselves seperate, their customs are different, they do not obey the kings laws
>
> their laws are different from all other people's laws

How does Haman appeal to King Ahasuerus's self-interest?

- verse 8

> they keep themselves seperatet.
> they do not obey the king's laws

- verse 9

> if it pleases the king.
> I will pay 10,000 talents of silver to those who do the work to bring it into the kings treasury
>
> - bribey

Annual Calendar at the Time of Esther		
	Ancient Month	**Modern Month**
1st Month	Nisan	March–April
2nd Month	Lyyar	April–May
3rd Month	Sivan	May–June
4th Month	Tammuz	June–July
5th Month	Ab	July–August
6th Month	Elul	August–September
7th Month	Tishri	September–October
8th Month	Marchesvan	October–November
9th Month	Chislev	November–December
10th Month	Tebeth	December–January
11th Month	Shebat	January–February
12th Month	Adar	February–March

✦ The Persians weren't the only ancient society to practice casting lots. It was customary even in Israel when God's guidance was needed. Read Proverbs 16:33. What light does that proverb cast on what's happening here in Persia?

" The lot is cast into the lap but its every decision is from the LORD

God is sovereign over every event all the time big or small"

✦ King Ahasuerus gives Haman his signet ring, indicating his approval of Haman's plot. Haman now has unlimited power to do as he wishes. To possess the king's signet ring was to possess the authority of the king himself. What fact about Haman's background is repeated in verse 10, and what is it meant to emphasize?

Haman, son of Hammedatha the Agagite (King Agag) consequences of disobedience

4. HAMAN'S EVIL EDICT (3:12–15)

Nisan, the month in which Haman had cast the lots, was when the Jewish Passover was traditionally celebrated, and the thirteenth day of the month—when Haman issued his edict to destroy the Jews—was the eve of this important holiday. Passover commemorates God's deliverance of his people from slavery in Egypt way back in the days of Moses. The point here is that Haman's plot to wipe out God's people is set in motion just as the Jews are preparing to celebrate the greatest and most miraculous deliverance in their history. (Passover is a vitally significant event in Bible history, so it would be helpful to build in a few extra minutes of study time this week to learn a bit about it in Exodus 12:1–32.)

✦ Describe the spread of Haman's edict. Who received it, and how far did it reach?

Kings highest officers, the governors, the respective provinces + nobles of each province in their own language + script —

— sent by messengers + every province + proclaimed to all peoples)

✦ What was used to signify the authority behind the edict?

it was sealed with the King's signet ring

✦ What specific instructions were included in the letters that accompanied the edict?

orders that ALL Jews: men, women, children *young & old*
must be killed /slaughtered /annihilated
in a single day

✦ Esther 3 ends with a contrast. Identify the contrast and what it conveys about

· King Ahasuerus:

sat down & drank

· Haman:

sat down & drank

· Citizens of Susa:

confused / perplexed   "fell into confusion"
" The citizens of the empire knew Jewish people
who lived among them & caused no trouble/harm
& were good citizens.
The were perplexed that such a decree came forth
declaring the Jews as dangerous enemies

LET'S TALK

1. It's clear from the story so far that both King Ahasuerus and Haman crave respect, and they are both easily enraged when it is withheld. We witnessed the king's anger when Queen Vashti refused his demand, and now Haman's hatred flares for an entire people because one individual refuses to bow down to him. Their rage exposes not only their fragile, insecure hold on the respect they crave, but also how very deep that craving goes. It rules them, driving their passions and plans. Do you harbor a strong desire—a craving—for respect? If not respect, is there some other longing that tends to rule you—perhaps a longing for love or admiration? Are there ways in which you try to demand it from the people in your life and, if so, what is the typical outcome?

2. Evil against God's people has been plotted ever since the serpent brought down Adam and Eve in the garden of Eden. We may not experience the life-threatening plots experienced by so many believers around the world, but we hear about these horrible happenings, and we wonder why God doesn't intervene more visibly. What gives you confidence when evil seems to triumph, as it does in Esther's story right now? Maybe you've experienced rejection or loss because you identify with God and his people. What can strengthen your faith when this happens? You might want to take a look at Matthew 10:27–31 and John 15:18–20; 16:33.

What gives me confidence when evil seems to
triumph is the RESURRECTION!!

John 16:33

"In this world you will have trouble & sorrows
But all that Jesus told His disciples (and tells
us in His Word) will give us peace in the midst
of tribulation because He has overcome the world

SUCH A TIME AS THIS

ESTHER 4:1-17

Confusion—that's where we were in our story at the end of last week. Haman had convinced King Ahasuerus that annihilating God's people, the Jews, was a good idea, so a decree was issued throughout the land that all the Jews far and near were to be killed at the end of the year. The news was unsettling, to say the least—not only for the Jews but for all the citizens dwelling in the capital city of Susa. After all, Jews and Persians had been coexisting for years, and while surely there were ethnic tensions and some suspicions and dislike, daily life moved along pretty well. The official edict against the Jews was a game changer, as Persians were ordered to turn against the Jews, many of whom were neighbors and friends. Overnight, daily life had become dark and unsettling.

1. MORDECAI EXPOSED (4:1-3)

Mordecai has changed too. When we met him back in week 2, we got the impression that he preferred to identify more as a Persian than as a Jew, at least publicly. For one thing, he'd advised his young ward, Esther, to keep her Jewish identity a secret. For another, his respected position in the city gates likely couldn't have happened unless he'd demonstrated zeal for all things Persian and loyalty to the empire. But once Haman came to power, Mordecai made his Jewish identity known.

This was a real risk for someone in Mordecai's position. Remember why God's people were living in Persia in the first place—they'd been captured and forcibly brought to this region decades before. So not only did some dislike the Jews for ethnic reasons; others saw them as weak and inferior. Acknowledging his Jewishness could very well have cost Mordecai his respected position at the gate.

✦ Mordecai has gone from hiding his Jewish identity (Esther 2), to admitting it to his colleagues at the city gates (Esther 3), to what we see here in Esther 4. What further risk does Mordecai take in verse 2?

coming near the city gate in sackloth and ashes)

✦ Up until now, God's people have fared quite well in Persia. We remember that some had returned to Jerusalem, their homeland, but many had not. We aren't told why, but it could be that a return to Jerusalem meant leaving behind Persian comforts and participating in the difficult task of rebuilding all that had been destroyed years before. For that reason, perhaps it was just easier to stay put. After all, some likely reasoned, they'd had little trouble living as Jews among the Persians. But overnight all that changed. How do the Jews respond to the edict?

mourning tearing their clothes) fasted wept + wailed

✦ In those days people not only wept and fasted to show grief but also tore their clothes and covered themselves in ashes. Certainly Haman's evil plan was cause for great sorrow, but the outpouring of emotion here likely involved more than just tears and torn clothes. In the chart below, note what prompted other occasions of God's people mourning and what happened as a result.

Who Mourns	Reason for Mourning	Activities of Mourning	Outcome of Mourning
King David (2 Samuel 12:15–24)	*God's pending judgment for David's sin*	• *Fasting* • *Praying that punishment will be averted*	*Acceptance of God's will*
God's unfaithful people (Joel 2:1-2; 12-13)	The day of the LORD was upon them darkness, gloom, blackness	fasting, weeping, mourning, tearing clothes	Return to the LORD
Christians (James 4:4-10)	over my sin spiritual adultry	wash your hands purify your heart let there be tears, sorrow + deep grief let there be sadness + gloom HUMBLING	God will come close to you draw near - He will lift you up

🕊 What insights do we get from these passages that shed light on the mourning going on in Susa?

....

....

....

....

2. ESTHER'S DILEMMA (4:4-11)

Meanwhile, Esther has been tucked away in the king's palace, oblivious to the horrible fate planned for her people.

◆ What distresses Esther, and what does she do about it in verse 4?

That Mordecai was distressed & mourning, she sends clothes to him

◆ Esther's concern deepens when Mordecai refuses her attempt to help him. She calls for one of her attendants, Hathach, and orders him to go outside and find out why Mordecai is so upset. Mordecai brings Hathach up to speed and sends him back to Esther with a command. What does Mordecai want Esther to do?

To go to the king on behalf of the Jews

◆ Hathach is stuck in the middle! He relays to Esther all that Mordecai told him to say—the great dilemma facing God's people—but Esther sends Hathach right back to Mordecai with a dilemma of her own. What is Esther's dilemma, and why does she have reason for concern?

If she is not invited into the inner courts and the king hold out his scepter it would be a death sentence.

3. GOD KEEPS HIS PROMISES (4:12-14)

Mordecai listens as he is told of Esther's dilemma, but the risk she faces doesn't change his thinking. He is determined that the best way forward is for Esther to approach the king and make an appeal for the Jewish people. So he sends messengers back with a final word for Esther.

✢ The first point in Mordecai's final appeal is meant to open Esther's eyes to a particular reality (v. 13). What is it?

She will not be excluded from the decree just because she is in the palace

✢ What confidence does Mordecai express in verse 14?

God is going to deliver the Jews one way or another, if not through her than someone else. She was appointed queen for such a time as this

✣ The author of our story doesn't tell us the reason for Mordecai's confidence, but the very fact that he *is* confident indicates that life in Persia hasn't made him forget the promises of God. What promises do you see in the passages below? To whom were the promises made, and who receives the blessings promised?

	What Is Promised and to Whom?	Who Is Blessed?
Genesis 12:1-3	all the nations Abram land, legacy.	all the nations
2 Samuel 7:8-16	David security, A house a strong Kingdom Rest, fame	Israel
Isaiah 43:1-7	Jacob & security, freedom rescue - bring back to God Restoration	Israel,

✣ Taken together, how do those passages in the chart above provide the reason for Mordecai's confidence?

Mordecai knows Israel's history and God's providence & provision in preserving the nation, but that doesn't necessarily mean that he was godly or repentant?

✦ Mordecai was confident of God's deliverance, but he didn't know how it would play out. Read Galatians 1:3–4 and Colossians 1:13. How do these passages show us how Mordecai's confident words were ultimately fufilled?

As God had planned He rescued us, through the offering and sacrifice of His Son

– present evil age – the world apart from Christ

Mordecai is confident that the Jews will be delivered, but he warns Esther that if she refuses to step up, she herself will perish along with her family legacy. Mordecai's warning seems confusing at first. If the Jews are to be delivered, why won't Esther be included among them? One possibility is that God's promise of deliverance was made to the Jewish people as a whole; in other words, God didn't promise that each individual Jew would survive. Or maybe Mordecai was thinking of spiritual death rather than physical death. In other words, if Esther refuses to take this risk, <u>she is in effect choosing to disassociate from God's people and therefore from God himself.</u>

hiding or denying your identity as a Jew, denies God Himself because they are inseperably linked.

✦ Mordecai ends his final appeal to Esther with a question, something for her to ponder as she weighs the risks before her (vv. 13–14). What does Mordecai want her to realize about herself and, most likely, about God?

Esther is still obeying her "father" rather than her husband – She still taking orders from Mordecai

She is a Jew, if the nation is taken out, so is she.

4. ESTHER'S CHOICE (4:15–17)

Mordecai's appeal penetrates Esther's heart, and she makes her choice. She will risk her life on behalf of her people, the Jews. Entering the king's presence uninvited was prohibited and could mean certain death, unless the king was in the mood to show favor to the intruder. Esther is rightly frightened, because while the king has delighted in her company in times past, it seems his interest has cooled a bit, as he hasn't summoned her for an entire month. When she approaches, will she be viewed as a cherished wife or as a nuisance?

✦ To prepare to approach the king, Esther decides to fast. Who does she include in the fast, and what does her initiative indicate about her allegiances?

> She fasted, did not eat or drink in 3 days
> and instructed the Jews to do the same
> — Her allegiance was to her people, not necessarily
> her God.

*Thank you LORD, that in spite of my idolity and denying You,
Your will is still done. Your promises are irrevocable.*

✦ Esther is clear-headed and utterly realistic about the risk she is taking. What does she say that lets us know this?

> If I perish, I perish

More than the King decree

"Now is my soul troubled. And what shall I say?
'Father, save me from this hour'? But for this purpose
I have come to this hour. Father, glorify your name."
Then a voice came from heaven: "I have glorified it,
and I will glorify it again." . . . "Now is the judgment
of this world; now will the ruler of this world be cast
out. And I, when I am lifted up from the earth, will
draw all people to myself." (John 12:27–32)

Hmm... being a God and being a Jew were inseparably linked. To (hide) deny your nationality was to deny God also

⊗ Note: No prayer, "mourning", "fasting" but no prayer.

? Mordecai not in the will of God. He should have never been in Shushan. He should have returned to Jerusalem when Cyrus gave decree to return to homeland only a few went. The rest grew comfortable w/ persian ways

At the beginning of Esther 4, we noted the changes in Mordecai, and here at the end we can't help but notice even greater changes in Esther. The young woman who was accustomed to taking the path of least resistance has become a more mature woman who is willing to sacrifice her very life for the sake of God's people.

had a political position Mordecai

We noted earlier that Mordecai was confident of deliverance because God had promised long ago to preserve his people forever. Mordecai didn't have the full picture of how God would keep his promise, but we do: God kept it through Jesus. Like Esther, Jesus was willing to die to save God's people, but he did way more than Esther ever could have done. Read Jesus's words in John 12:27–28. What specifically in this last section of Esther 4 foreshadows Jesus's words here in John?

_____

_____

_____

LET'S TALK

1. Until this chapter, both Mordecai and Esther had been navigating two separate identities. They were Jews by birth, but they had been living as Persians. And by downplaying their Jewish heritage and entering wholeheartedly into Persian culture, both Esther and Mordecai had prospered greatly. Are you tempted to live out more than one identity? If so, what have you gained or hope to gain? Discuss how 1 John 2:15–17 speaks to this issue in general and to your own life in particular.

do not love the world or the things in the world, $$

_____

_____

2. Esther responds to the danger she faces with great courage: "If I perish, I perish" (v. 16). Like Esther, sometimes we find ourselves in situations requiring boldness and courage. It might be launching out in a specific path of costly obedience. Or maybe it's openly sharing our faith. Describe a time when you stepped out with Esther's kind of courage. What happened? Were you able to identify God's delivering hand in that situation?

RISE AND FALL

ESTHER 5:1-14

No doubt Esther was physically weak after her three-day fast. We aren't told how Esther was actually feeling, but we can be confident that if she sought the Lord during her fast, his strength was now sustaining her as she made final preparations to approach her husband, King Ahasuerus. Up until now Esther has been a compliant young woman, eager to please and win the favor of others. But now we can detect confidence and a good bit of assertiveness, and also a knack for good timing. As you read through the chapter, notice how Esther continues to change as the story unfolds.

1. IN THE PRESENCE OF ROYALTY (5:1–5)

On the third day, when the fast was complete, Esther prepares to see the king by putting on her "royal robes," and she bravely sets out for the king's palace, where King Ahasuerus is sitting on his throne. Little is known about women's clothing in ancient Persia because women lived much of their lives in seclusion. But we know that Persian men of royal status wore the color purple, so maybe queens did too. Purple was a color of nobility in ancient Israel also, and in the Bible purple is associated with two women of noble character: the wise woman of Proverbs 31 (v. 22) and Lydia the seller of purple cloth in Acts 16:13–15.

✦ Why do you think Esther chose to wear her royal robes to go see the king?

maybe to remind him she was queen or to enhance her beauty further

The king extends his royal scepter, and Esther reaches out to touch it. A scepter is a sort of staff that monarchs hold in their hand to symbolize their power and authority. King Ahasuerus's scepter was made of gold. We aren't told why Esther touched the scepter, but perhaps it was a way of connecting with him, royalty with royalty. Esther has come in her queenly attire; she is not some nameless concubine but the queen of Persia! She is shaping how she wants the king to view her before she even opens her mouth to speak to him. And from the king's reaction—he calls her "Queen Esther"—it seems that her intuition about how to approach him is working as she'd hoped.

✦ What does King Ahasuerus offer Esther?

half the kingdom

Esther's response to the king's offer seems surprising at first. Why was she passing up a golden opportunity to save the lives of her people, the Jews? The king had vowed to give her what she wanted, so he'd have to spare the lives of the Jews or risk losing face. King Ahasuerus has opened wide the door for Esther to plead for the lives of her people. But Esther takes a different approach.

✦ What does Esther say to the king?

come back with Haman tomorrow to another banquet

This was a shrewd move on Esther's part. She knows from experience that King Ahasuerus has a fragile ego and can be easily manipulated. If she were to blurt out her real request so soon, the king might grant her petition, but his advisors could just as easily talk him out of it later. So Esther wins more time with her husband to reestablish connection and trust by inviting him, along with his right-hand man Haman, to dinner.

2. ESTHER'S FIRST FEAST (5:6–8)

The king and Haman have had their fill of Esther's feast and are enjoying an after-dinner wine. And surely the king is curious at this point. He knows Esther risked her life to approach him earlier that day, something she likely wouldn't have done just for the chance to dine with him. So the king presses Esther to speak her mind.

How does Esther's response to the king in verses 7–8 differ from her earlier response in verse 4? Note the differences you see.

in 7-8 she turns on the charm but she makes it more about what "pleases" the king

she's appealing to his pleasure

3. A PORTRAIT OF A FOOL (5:9–14)

The drama focuses on Haman in this section, and we are able to see a bit about his life—and also his heart. He leaves Esther's feast in a jubilant mood. After all, he's the only man who had been invited besides the king, and now he feels even more confident and secure in the king's inner circle.

What changes Haman's mood so suddenly and how does it change?

Seeing Mordecai and his continued refusal to bow down

✦ Mordecai really gets under Haman's skin. We're told that Haman "restrained himself and went home" (v. 10). What does he do once he gets home?

> He brags / boasts of all that was given to him & how he was honored by the king & queen but sulks because of all one man, Mordecai

✦ What does Haman tell his friends and family in verses 12–13, and what does this reveal about Haman's heart, about what matters most to him?

> His pride ~~was~~ complained that Mordecai would not bow down —
>
> His heart is empty because he doesn't want God, he will never be satisfied because he is looking to man for sats fac

all his discontent over one man

✦ What insights do we get about Haman from the following proverbs?

· Proverbs 14:29   He is never satisfied discontent.

> a temper shows how foolish we are

His empty/ discontent

" Ec. 5:10

He who loves money will never be satisfied with money, nor he who loves abundance with its income: this too is vanity.

· Proverbs 29:10

> blood thirsty people hate blameless people

A fool vents all his feelings but a wise man builds them up

Proverbs 29:11

> Fools vent their anger

➤ Is. 65:13 ✝
"Therefore thus says the LORD GOD
Behold my servants → will eat
but you will be hungry

Ec. 6:7 All a man's labor is for his mouth and yet his appetite is never satisfied"

The gallows and the agonizing cruelty of it was made because of the destroying destructive power of hatred. The same hatred that had Jesus crucified

◆ What do we learn in this section about Haman's wife, Zeresh?

She is just as concerned (pridefully) about her husband's standing

Instrument in the Redeemer's Hand.

The edict against the Jews won't go into effect for several months, but Zeresh has an idea. Why wait to put an end to Mordecai? Zeresh, with the backing of family friends, sets out a detailed plan to hang this bothersome Jew. The gallows she outlines will be tall enough so that everyone in the city will witness the fate of Mordecai and learn a valuable lesson about what happens to people who refuse to bow to Haman.

◆ Summarize how the hidden hand of God works through the people in this chapter to move the story forward. Note which of these people initiate and which ones are passive responders.

· Esther:

· Looking ahead, Esther's hesitation to ask for her people at the first banquet gave an extra night for King Xerxes to have the dream that would exalt Mordecai and destroy Haman

· King Ahasuerus:

passive

· Haman: *passive*

Proverbs 27:20 " Sheol & abaddon are never satisfied
Nor are the eyes of man ever satisfied

" Behold, my servants will drink, but you will be thirsty
Behold, my servants will rejoice, but you will be put to shame."

· Zeresh:

LET'S TALK

1. Commentator Karen Jobes summarizes what we've seen of Esther in this chapter: "Esther assumes the dignity and power of her royal position only after she claims her true identity as a woman of God."[3] There is a principle here for our own lives. How has identifying yourself as a follower of Christ transformed you and your life in tangible ways?

testimony of being catholic

2. Haman's wife, Zeresh, encouraged her husband to gratify his sinful cravings and commit great evil. This isn't the first time in Scripture that a wife has enticed her husband to sin. Job's wife counseled Job to sin (Job 2:9), and the wicked Queen Jezebel did the same thing to her husband, King Ahab (1 Kings 21:1–16). These wives violated God's design for marriage, which is, in part, the mutual upbuilding of both husband and wife. The same principle applies to all our relationships, as the apostle Paul writes: "Let no corrupting talk come out of your mouths, but only such as is good for building up, as fits the occasion, that it

may give grace to those who hear" (Ephesians 4:29). How do you use your personal gifts—mind, talent, energy, education, intuition, and spiritual discernment—to build up your relationships? How and when might you be tempted to use those gifts in ways that tear down rather than build up?

_____

_____

_____

_____

_____

_____

_____

_____

HAMAN'S VERY BAD DAY

ESTHER 6:1-14

Tossing and turning—it was one of those nights when King Ahasuerus couldn't sleep. We know from the historian Herodotus that this wasn't the first time the king suffered a bout of insomnia. Whatever the underlying source—indigestion from the rich food at Esther's feast perhaps, or too much wine—whatever the cause, King Ahasuerus couldn't sleep. Queen Esther was most likely the cause of his restlessness on this particular night. The king knew that his wife was clearly troubled by something. After all, she'd risked her life to get his attention and ask him for favor. But what favor—companionship over dinner? There had to be more! After dinner, he'd encouraged her to tell him, but she'd put him off again with the promise of another feast. She'd promised to tell him her wish after this second dinner. All this mystery—no wonder he couldn't sleep!

1. ONE SLEEPLESS NIGHT (6:1-3)

The entire story of Esther begins to turn because of what happens in verse 1: "On that night the king could not sleep." Whatever the cause of the king's insomnia, the providential hand of God was controlling it.

✦ How does each of the following passages deepen our understanding of how God works in the seemingly random details of life—not just kings' lives but ours too?

· Psalm 139:15–16

Before there was a single day of my life, you knew me, You saw me being formed in my mother's womb, every moment/day of my life was laid out before a single day passed

Esther's
3 days of
fasting
prov. 16:3
commit your
works to the
LORD +
your plans
will succeed
when you
follow His
will +
guidance

· Proverbs 16:1

The plans and reflections of the heart belong to man, but the wise answer of the tongue is from the LORD

· Proverbs 16:9

We make our plans but the LORD determines our steps

· Proverbs 19:21

" Many plans are in man's mind but it is the LORD's purpose for him that will stand.
" You can make many plans, but the LORD's purpose will prevail .

· Proverbs 20:24

"man's steps are ordered & ordained by the LORD, how then can a man fully understand his ways?"

"The LORD directs our steps so why try to understand everything along the way .

Pr: 16: 4
" The LORD has made everything for its own purpose, even the wicked for the day of evil "

· Proverbs 21:1

"The King's heart is like a stream of water
directed by the LORD; He guides it wherever He
pleases"

· Acts 17:24–28

IN HIM
WE LIVE
AND MOVE
AND
EXIST

He gives life and breath to all people. He
has NO NEEDS. He made from one man (Adam)
every nation & determined their appointed
times & boundaries of their lands & territories
SO They WOULD SEEK HIM

· Romans 11:36

" For from Him [all things
originate] and through Him
[all things live and exist],
and to Him are all things
[directed]. To Him be the
glory and honor forever, Amen"

Herodotus

Herodotus was a well-educated Greek historian, most likely from an upscale family. His most famous work, *The Histories*, gives us one of the earliest accounts of life in the Persian Empire. Herodotus lived from about 484–425 BC, which falls within the window of King Ahasuerus's rule and the lives of Esther and Mordecai.

· Colossians 1:16

" *For through Him (Christ) God created everything in the heavenly realms and on earth. He made the things we can see and the things we can't see such as thrones, Kingdoms rulers, and authorities in the unseen world. Everything was created through Him and for Him.*

✦ Rather than toss and turn the night away, the king did what many of us do on sleepless nights—he decided to read. Specifically, the king asked for "the book of memorable deeds," in which were recorded all the important happenings in Persia. The book was a log of people and places, payments and gifts. What does King Ahasuerus discover as he reads?

Mordecai exposed a plan to take the King's life.

Rewarding citizens for patriotic acts and deeds that benefited the king was vitally important in those days, when authority figures were regularly overthrown or assassinated. Honoring faithful citizens helped ensure their loyalty. So as dawn approaches, the king is understandably perturbed when he discovers an oversight.

2. RISE AND FALL (6:4-11)

As the sun rises, we see the guiding hand of God again. After finding out that Mordecai's earlier heroism has gone unrewarded, King Ahasuerus wants to remedy the oversight as soon as possible, so he looks around the court for any trusted advisor to guide him.

✦ Where do you see God's providence guiding the events that unfold in this scene?

> Gods providence Kept Ester from revealing what she wanted on day 1 at the banquet. The King had a sleepless night and asked for a book. There were MANY Books of events. The ONE was chosen and the book was opened to that particular event.

✦ In what way is Haman's view of himself skewed? How is this reflected in his description of how a civic hero should be honored (vv. 7–9)?

> who would the king like to honor more than me.

✦ Why would Haman view the king's order in verse 10 as just about the worst thing he could think of?

> The honor he craved and coveted from Mordecai is now coming from him to Mordecai.

The Providence of God

God's works of providence are his most holy, wise, and powerful preserving and governing of all his creatures; ordering them, and all their actions, to his own glory.
—*Westminster Larger Catechism*

3. NO WAY OUT (6:12–14)

The fanfare has ended. Mordecai returns to his work at the king's gate, and Haman heads home.

In this section we see Haman quickly on the move, but the pace of his life had already begun to change, even in the last chapter. Note in each case, below, what caused Haman to hurry.

- 5:4–5

To go to the first banquet of the queen, King summoned him to come quickly

- 6:10

Quick, take the robes and King's horse and do all that you spoke for Mordecai

- 6:12

quickly went home dejected and humiliated

- 6:14

quickly taken to the second banquet

✦ What impression do you think the author of Esther is trying to make here?

He's not in control anymore

Back at home, Haman pours out his humiliation to his wife, Zeresh, and his friends. They realize what Haman can't yet see—God's people, the Jews, seem to be protected by a hidden yet powerful hand.

Isaiah 54:17

✦ What, according to Haman's people, not only will likely happen but is already happening?

evil Plans against the Jews will never prosper and if (God's people) US — Thank You LORD you continuing to oppose, it will be fatal to the one against them

✦ How is Haman's approach to the king's court at the end of Esther 6 (v. 14) different from his approach at the beginning (v. 4)?

?? Haman arrived to the king's court on his own
. . Eunuchs quickly brought them to banquet.

Isaiah 54:17
" No weapon forged against you will prevail, and you will refute every tongue that accuses you. This is the heritage of the servants of the LORD, and this is their vindication from Me declares the LORD."

LET'S TALK

1. If you have ever experienced a sleepless night, it's likely you know the unsettled loneliness and anxious thoughts that characterize those hours. But it is in the ordinary, mundane events of daily life—and often the most frustrating ones—that God is working out his purposes. It was true of King Ahasuerus, and it is true of us. Can you look back at a seemingly random event in your life and recognize now how God was at work in it?

2. The Persians didn't quite know what to make of these foreigners, the Jews, who'd settled in their midst. How are we as Christians viewed by the unbelievers we live among? What do we contribute to their view of God by how we live our day-to-day lives in our homes, schools, offices, and communities?

EXPOSURE!

ESTHER 7:1-10

Food and wine, soft music floating on the air, and conversational banter—no doubt Haman's wounded pride has been soothed as Esther's second feast begins to wind down. And King Ahasuerus, impatient to hear Queen Esther's wish, leans in for an answer. His tongue loosened from wine, he asks again, "What is your wish, Queen Esther?" The time has come. Esther can delay no longer. And from this point on, events move at lightning speed, even faster than last week, as we saw Haman hurry here and there.

1. THE TRUTH REVEALED (7:1-6)

King Ahasuerus wants to know why Esther has prepared two feasts for him and his chief of staff, Haman. And to encourage her to open up, he repeats his earlier promise to give her up to half his kingdom.

✦ Esther begins to pour out her heart in verse 3. What qualifications does she mention in her response to the king, and what does she ask for?

The pleasure of the King and and the favor of the King

✦ What does Esther begin to expose in verse 3?

that she is a Jew

Esther reveals the plot against the Jews in verse 4. And when she speaks of the Jews being "sold," she exposes Haman's earlier offer to the king (see Esther 3:9) for what it was—bribery.

✦ Review Esther's carefully chosen words in verses 3–4 and summarize the various ways she appeals to the king's self-interest.

if it pleases him, his time is so important to be disturbed with trivial matters

✦ It is evident in the king's outraged response to Esther's appeal that he has known very little about Haman's edict against the Jews. The king had simply rubber-stamped the edict when his trusted advisor had pitched it to him, because it seemed in his own best interests to give the go-ahead. But as to those who would actually be affected by it, well, he hadn't bothered to investigate. And even here, in verse 5, he again doesn't ask for details. Why, then, is the king so outraged?

We can almost feel sorry for Haman, as we imagine the horror he felt at being so suddenly exposed. He too is discovering something he had not known previously—Queen Esther is Jewish and therefore among those doomed to death by his edict. Nor had Haman known of her close affiliation with Mordecai.

2. WHAT GOES AROUND COMES AROUND (7:7-10)

King Ahasuerus is reeling, not primarily from wine but from Esther's shocking revelation. Haman, the advisor he'd chosen to trust, has manipulated him into a plot that would result in the death of his very own queen! (The king, of course, doesn't know the whole story, that Haman too had been in the dark about Esther's Jewish identity.) So upset is the king that he storms out of the banqueting hall, leaving Esther and Haman alone.

Haman is now in a no-win situation. He risks inflaming the king's wrath even more by lingering in the dining room because, in Persian culture, no man could be alone with the king's wife or his concubines except for the king himself. So, according to custom, when the king got up and left, Haman should have left as well. On the other hand, leaving would make him look guilty, as if he were running away to avoid facing up to Esther's accusations.

✦ What does King Ahasuerus see when he comes in from the palace garden, and how does he interpret it?

> He saw Haman, he was kneeling on the floor
> before Esth, the King thought he
> was assaulting Esth

✦ Haman's face is quickly covered, symbolizing that he stands condemned, and immediately after, Harbona the eunuch speaks to the king. What does Harbona suggest, and how does he speak about Mordecai?

> That the gallows Haman made to empale
> Mordecai "the man who saved the King"
> be used on Haman

✦ Harbona has a favored place in the king's court, being one of the eunuchs who serves in the king's presence. This is the second time Harbona has appeared in our story. He was in attendance at the feast that King Ahasuerus hosted for the citizens of Susa and was among those commanded to fetch Queen Vashti when the king wanted to show her off. Given his position so near to the king, Harbona surely knew a good bit about Persian affairs of state and about the king himself. As we consider his advice to the king here and the way he phrased it, what can we surmise about his view of the situation and the people involved—a view likely shared by others close to the king?

✦ What finally calms the king's anger?

the ordering of the execution of Haman

When we read that Haman was hanged on the gallows, we most likely picture a rope with a noose at the end, hanging down from a tall perch. But when a criminal was hanged in ancient Persia, it typically involved not a rope around the neck but a stake thrust through the torso from the bottom up. It was a gruesome way to die. We don't know exactly how Haman was executed, nor do we need to know. Haman's rapid political rise and his even faster fall are what the author wants us to see—overshadowed, of course, by the hidden hand of God, who is governing every detail of the unfolding story.

God has not destined us for wrath, but to obtain salvation through our Lord Jesus Christ, who died for us so that whether we are awake or asleep we might live with him. (1 Thessalonians 5:9–10)

What light do the following passages shed on God's presence in the book of Esther up to this point in the story?

· Deuteronomy 32:39

> God is the one who Kills & saves and gives life - He is the one who wounds - He is always sovereign in control

· Job 42:1–2

> God can do anything and no one can stop Him

· Psalm 75:6–7

> God alone judges - He decides who rises and who falls

· Daniel 2:20–22

> God has ALL wisdom & power, He controls the course of world events He removes Kings & sets up other Kings, He gives wisdom to the wise and Knowledge to the scholars, He reveals deep and mysterious things and knows what lies hidden in darkness though He is surrounded by light

· Romans 13:1

> All authority and all who are in authority comes from God

The very last thing we're told in Esther 7 is that after Haman was lifted up on the gallows, the king's anger was calmed. The author of Esther couldn't have known the degree to which his telling of the story foreshadowed something so much greater. Like Haman, Jesus Christ was lifted up—not on a gallows but on a cross. Unlike Haman, Jesus was condemned for guilt not his own. He paid for our sin—the guilt of all God's people in every age and for all time. And once Christ's work on the cross was finished, God's righteous anger against our sin, like King Ahasuerus's anger, abated.

> *Haman sought to kill God's people and lost his own life. Jesus died for God's people and won for them life everlasting.*

Despite Esther's powerful plea and Haman's demise in this chapter, the evil plot he'd set in motion lingers. What danger still hangs over God's people?

The decree to kill all Jews

LET'S TALK

1. Reflect on Esther's plan to expose Haman and the means she used to carry it out. Where can you detect some womanly wisdom in Esther's approach? How do you handle personal crises or circumstances in which you are desperate for help?

_____

2. Haman was so arrogant that he walked right into Esther's trap. Pride blinds us to reality, most especially to reality about ourselves. Haman's pride was his downfall, and it cost him his life. We can imagine the terror he felt as his final hours unfolded. We never want to know firsthand what that feels like! But we all struggle with pride in one way or another, even as we seek to grow in humility. How, according to 1 Peter 5:5–8, do we humble ourselves?

by humbling myself as I relate to others)
by giving all my worries to God, my worry is
a form of pride because I somehow feel like
I have lost control — worry is distrust,
worry desires to be in control —
God is in control and He cares about me
I need His MIGHTY POWER to even humble myself.

A GREAT REVERSAL

ESTHER 8:1-17

Peace has been restored in the king's court—at least, for the moment. Haman has been executed, thereby removing the threat to Queen Esther. But the greater threat remains—the edict against the Jews. In just eight months' time, God's people will be wiped out. Something must be done, and it must be done quickly, but what? Royal edicts in Persia, signed and sealed by the king, were irreversible.

1. TAKING DOWN AND SETTING UP (8:1-2)

The exposure and execution of Haman has removed a threat to King Ahasuerus's authority, not to mention a humiliating insult to the king. Delighting in his restored sense of power and kingly dignity, Ahasuerus gives Haman's estate—all his belongings and money—to Esther, which he had the right to do with the property of a condemned criminal.

✦ What brings Mordecai to the king?

The fact that he was related to Esther

✦ Note below the reversals that occur in these opening verses.

· Verse 1:

Esther receives all of Haman's property

· Verse 2:

the signet ring & position of authority that once belonged to Haman now belongs to Mordecai

2. A NEW DAY AND A NEW WAY (8:3-8)

The edict against the Jews remains in force, so Esther must once again take a great risk and plead for the lives of her people. Will the king allow her to speak in his presence? He does, once again holding out to her his golden scepter.

✦ In what way is Esther's appeal to the king different here from her initial appeal in 5:1-4?

she implored w/ tears.

if it pleases

if I have found favor
if it seems right.

if I have found favor

if I am pleasing in your sight

◆ What does Esther ask the king to do, and on what conditions does she base her appeal (v. 5)?

she asks him to counteract/reverse Haman's edict —
— if I found favor – if I please you, if you
think it's right

In her appeal to the king, Esther refers to Haman as "the Agagite," even though the king probably did not know (or care) what this meant. But it's important! If you recall, a people called the Amalekites, which included a king named Agag, had been marked by God as enemies of the Jews way back in the days of Moses. Haman was a descendant of these wicked Amalekites, and although Haman himself is gone, his edict is still in force, which means that the Amalekites are continuing to haunt God's people. And Esther cannot bear it.

Likely King Ahasuerus is sighing a bit as he listens to Esther his queen. He is fond of her, and he finds her desirable, but her pleas have caused him no small amount of trouble, and now she is at it again. Doesn't she realize that an edict once issued could not be revoked? Were he to attempt it, he'd look like a ridiculously weak leader. His exasperation seems evident in his initial reply here: "Behold, I have given Esther the house of Haman, and they have hanged him on the gallows, because he intended to lay hands on the Jews" (v. 7). In other words, *"What more do you want from me? I have given you all that belonged to Haman after putting him to death."*

But wait a minute—look again at verse 7, where the king says that Haman was hanged "because he intended to lay hands on the Jews." Did you notice that the king puts a bit of spin on his words here? If we look back at the wording of Esther's plea in 7:3–4 and then at the rapid unfolding of events that culminated in Haman's death, nowhere do we see the king motivated by a desire to save the Jews. It was all about possible threats to himself—to his own rule. It's true that he'd been very upset at the threat to Esther, but even there, it was more about the fact that an attack on his queen was a personal affront to his kingly self.

✦ Still bound by the earlier edict crafted by Haman, the king nevertheless seeks to please his queen. What solution does he propose?

Mordecai + Esther write a new decree

3. KING AHASUERUS'S CLEVER SOLUTION (8:9–14)

The king's proposal is brilliant. The earlier edict to destroy the Jews cannot be revoked, but a new edict can be written that greatly reduces the terrible prospect of the earlier edict. According to the new edict, when the date comes for the Jews to be annihilated, the Jews can do whatever is necessary to defend themselves and preserve their lives. They won't be helpless sitting ducks. No wonder there is great rejoicing, which we see at the end of Esther 8. Although the official start date of Haman's evil edict was still months away, it's likely that persecution had already begun. Author Yoram Hazony paints this grim picture for us:

> The enemies of the Jews—not only the enemies of the Jewish people, but the enemies of every particular, individual Jew as well—swaggered about the public places, trumpeting their intentions in the face of every Jew who had ever insulted them, or edged them out for a public post, or charged them a price they believed to be too high . . . : "I will have your house when you are gone, Jew"; "I will have your daughter before she dies, Jew"; "I will dance on your grave, Jew." And worse. And with the taunting began acts of vandalism, of theft, of desecration, testing the Jews, humiliating them, preparing them.[4]

King Ahasuerus summons his scribes and assigns the drafting of the new edict to his newly installed chief advisor, Mordecai. In the box below, <u>underline</u> the *similarities* you see in the preparation of Mordecai's edict here and the preparation of Haman's from Esther 3. Then use the empty column to note the *differences* in the two accounts.

Haman's Edict (Esther 3:12–15)	Mordecai's Edict (Esther 8:9–14)	Differences
Then the king's scribes were summoned on the thirteenth day of the first month, and an edict, according to all that Haman commanded, was written to the king's satraps and to the governors over all the provinces and to the officials of all the peoples, to every province in its own script and every people in its own language.	The king's scribes were summoned at that time, in the third month, which is the month of Sivan, on the twenty-third day. And an edict was written, according to all that Mordecai commanded concerning the Jews, to the satraps and the governors and the officials of the provinces from India to Ethiopia, 127 provinces, to each province in its own script and to each people in its own language, and also to the Jews in their script and their language.	edict written by Mordecai, Haman – 13th day 23rd dg
It was written in the name of King Ahasuerus and sealed with the king's signet ring. Letters were sent by couriers to all the king's provinces with instruction to destroy, to kill, and to annihilate all Jews, young and old, women and children, in one day, the thirteenth day of the twelfth month, which is the month of Adar, and to plunder their goods. A copy of the document was to be issued as a decree in every province by proclamation to all the peoples to be ready for that day.	And he wrote in the name of King Ahasuerus and sealed it with the king's signet ring. Then he sent the letters by mounted couriers riding on swift horses that were used in the king's service, bred from the royal stud, saying that the king allowed the Jews who were in every city to gather and defend their lives, to destroy, to kill, and to annihilate any armed force of any people or province that might attack them, children and women included, and to plunder their goods, on one day throughout all the provinces of King Ahasuerus, on the thirteenth day of the twelfth month, which is the month of Adar.	sent swiftly on royal horses – annihilate – defend

Haman's Edict (Esther 3:12-15)	Mordecai's Edict (Esther 8:9-14)	Differences
The couriers went out hurriedly by order of the king, and the decree was issued in Susa the citadel. And the king and Haman sat down to drink, but the city of Susa was thrown into confusion.	A copy of what was written was to be issued as a decree in every province, being publicly displayed to all peoples, and the Jews were to be ready on that day to take vengeance on their enemies. So the couriers, mounted on their swift horses that were used in the king's service, rode out hurriedly, urged by the king's command. And the decree was issued in Susa the citadel.	

How would you summarize the gist of the new edict?

The jews could prepare for & have support for the attack

4. JOY AND GLADNESS (8:15-17)

Joy is the dominant note of this final section. The new decree has been issued, and like all decrees bearing the seal of the king's ring, it could never be revoked. God's people were free to defend themselves against their enemies, and they had all the government support they'd need.

✦ How is Mordecai presented to us here?

as royal authority

✦ What words does the author use to describe the mood among God's people throughout the land of Persia?

light, gladness, joy honor

✦ How did the Jews celebrate this momentous occasion?

by feasting and proclaiming a holiday

✦ How did Persian citizens respond to the new edict?

*many of the people of the land
became "Jews" –*

*"They saw God working on behalf of His
people & they wanted a relationship
with God"*

✦ Identify the reversals in the passages below.

· 3:15 reversed in 8:15

Shushan went from perplexed to celebrating

· 4:1 reversed in 8:15

Mordecai went from sackcloth & ashes to royal robes

· 4:3 reversed in 8:16–17

mourning, weeping to light & joy and gladness.

LET'S TALK

1. The book of Esther is gory—it's okay to acknowledge this reality. If we're honest, sometimes we struggle to understand why God allows such violence, especially when victims include women and children, as is the case here in the new edict drafted by Mordecai. It's not that God loves violence; it's that he hates sin! And the truth is, everyone—men, women, and children—are deserving of death and destruction because of sin. Karen Jobes writes, "From the beginning of time, God's war has been against sin and evil. . . . We seem to want God to destroy sin and evil but leave people alone. However, sin and evil do not exist apart from beings who sin and beings who do evil."[5]

Do you minimize or excuse your sin? Consider how the violence we've seen in Esther (with more to come) opens our eyes to the horror of sin and where sin inevitably leads. How does this impact your understanding of Jesus Christ and his gospel? (You might want to take a quick look at John 1:21.)

2. As we consider all the reversals in this chapter, we can't help but recognize the powerful hand of God orchestrating these changes. There's simply no other way these things could have happened. He is the God of reversals, delighting to raise the low and strengthen the weak. In what area of your life does this aspect of God's character personally impact your faith and give you hope? You might also want to consider Hannah (1 Sam. 2:2–5) and Mary (Luke 1:46–55), two women who experienced the "reversing power" of God.

DELIVERANCE

ESTHER 9:1-19

The dreaded day arrives. Haman's edict goes into effect, and those who hate God's people rise up to destroy them. But the newer edict also kicks in—the one crafted by Mordecai and Esther—which allows the Jews to do whatever is necessary to defend themselves. So on the thirteenth day of Adar, ethnic war breaks out in the city of Susa and in all the provinces in Persia. The outcome is sure, though—not because God's people are stronger than their enemies, but because God always keeps his promises.

1. POWER SHIFT (9:1-5)

The first sentence of Esther 9 pretty well sums up the entire book of Esther:

> Now in the twelfth month, which is the month of Adar, on the thirteenth day of the same, when the king's command and edict were about to be carried out, on the very day when the enemies of the Jews hoped to gain the mastery over them, the reverse occurred: the Jews gained mastery over those who hated them. (Esther 9:1)

◆ Last week we focused on the reversals in the book of Esther; so many of them occur in chapter 8! But what does this first verse of chapter 9 pinpoint as the overarching reversal of the entire story?

2 decrees second, reversing the first

The enemies of the

The Jews overpower their enemies

◆ Why, according to verse 2, were the enemies of the Jews unable to prevail?

Because everyone feared them

Roman 8:31 "what shall we say to these things? If God is for us, who can be against us?"

◆ Strengthening the Jews were all the Persian officials who came to help them. Why, according to verses 3–4, did these leaders side with the Jews?

for fear of Mordecai, he became more & more powerful and his fame spread

◆ We are told that the Jews "struck all their enemies with the sword, killing and destroying them, and did as they pleased to those who hated them" (v. 5). According to the edict authored by Mordecai (see 8:11), what were the terms under which the Jews could engage in such killing?

They were allowed to take the plunder

They could defend themselves

2. A BLOODY DAY (9:6-10)

In verses 6–10 we learn what occurred within the city limits of Susa. Among the many killed were Haman's ten sons, and the author even tells us their names. Perhaps that's because Haman had taken great pride in his sons and boasted about them (see 5:11). Writing their names was also a symbolic way of blotting out the entire history of Haman, including his family members.

Given the number of Jewish enemies killed within city limits, a significant bit of "plunder"—money and possessions and livestock belonging to the deceased—was there for the taking. And the Jews were permitted to take it, according to Mordecai's edict (see 8:11). Yet here we're told in verse 10—and again in verses 15 and 16—that the Jews left the plunder alone. Clearly the author of Esther wants us to note this detail since it is mentioned three times! This is one of those places in the Bible where we find a powerful connection to another part of the Bible, and it's one way that we can see how the whole Bible is not a bunch of separate stories—it's actually one big story.

During the course of our study, we've taken note of a longtime enemy of God's people, the Amalekites. They factor into our Esther study because Haman and his sons were descendants of these Amalekites. Because the Amalekite people had been extraordinarily vicious in how they treated God's people, God had promised way back, centuries before Esther, that he would completely blot them out (Exodus 17:14).

✦ Years and years after God made that promise but long before Esther's time, you might recall that God commanded Israel's King Saul to destroy the Amalekites in battle. Review what happened that day in 1 Samuel 15:1–23. Based on what you read there, how is the Jews' refusal to take plunder here another reversal?

They did not want anything associated w/ the evildoers

3. ESTHER'S WISHES (9:11-15)

From the safety of his palace, King Ahasuerus calmly discusses the bloodshed going on in the city streets outside. It's like he's discussing a sporting event! And then he does what he so often does when he is in a good mood—he offers to bless his wife, Queen Esther. This time, however, the offer is a bit different.

- In times past, the king's generosity was offered to Esther in response to her pleas. Here, he initiates. What does this seem to indicate about Esther's place in the king's life and court?

  He respected her and saw how Mighty her God is, He gave her some authority

  respect, honor authority

- What two wishes does Esther present to King Ahasuerus?

  let Haman's sons be hanged and another day of battle

Esther gets a lot of criticism for these two wishes. Her first desire, that the Jews be granted one more day of self-defense in Susa, seems unnecessary in light of the fact that the enemy has been virtually crushed already. Is her wish for an extra day of killing simply revenge for months of terrorism by those who hated God's people? The request makes her seem cold and mean. Some wonder if her rising status and growing power had changed her from a soft, compliant girl into a brutal woman. The author of the story doesn't make any moral judgment about Esther's actions or words, so we simply don't know. But it's just as likely that her request wasn't mean-spirited but simply pragmatic, because, as the king had just noted, they could only guess at the number of casualties in the outlying provinces. Another day of battle might enable the Jews to defend against any rebel Persians determined to slip into Susa to harm God's people. As for her second request, that Haman's deceased sons be hanged on the gallows for all to see, that was likely meant to serve as a warning to those who might still have ideas about harming the Jews.

✦ What happens with Esther's wishes?

both are granted

It's difficult to read about wars and bloodshed, especially in the Bible. And the mass killings commanded by God are especially challenging to understand. That's because Christians today don't engage in holy wars. In Old Testament times, God set apart and purified a certain people—the Jews—for himself, and he commanded that unholy people who threatened to destroy God's relationship with his special people had to be wiped out. That's what we mean by "holy war."

We must keep in mind that God, in mandating such killing, wasn't condemning innocent people. Throughout the Bible we are told that those killed in these wars were ripe for judgment. And it's not as if God's own people were any less sinful. It's purely that God set his love on them and chose to spare them. The apostle Paul tells us:

> All have sinned and fall short of the glory of God, and are justified by his grace
> as a gift, through the redemption that is in Christ Jesus. (Romans 3:23–24)

When Paul writes that we are "justified," he means that we are made right with God through Jesus's payment for our sins on the cross. And that work of Jesus applies not only to people who came after Jesus, but also to all God's people who lived before Jesus came and took on human flesh. Jesus's death and resurrection changed the nature of how wars for holiness are fought and how God's enemies are conquered.

✦ Describe this change from what you see in the passages below:

· Matthew 28:18–20

share the gospel
all authority is Jesus'

· Ephesians 6:10–18

our war is invisible but powerfully real.
We cannot fight it with physical weapons

4. TIME TO CELEBRATE (9:16–19)

For the first time, we learn what's happened outside the city of Susa. The Jews were victorious in the outlying provinces too. And then we get a breakdown of who did what on particular days.

🔸 We recall that the edicts—both Haman's and Mordecai's—went into effect on Adar 13. And both of these edicts were valid for just that one day. But then Esther requested another edict to carry out a second day of battle within the city of Susa. Sort through the dates and events in verses 16–19 and complete the chart below, filling in what happened on these specific days.

Date	Jews in Susa	Jews in Persian Provinces
Adar 13	Battled the enemy	Battled the enemy
Adar 14	Battled the enemy	*Rested/celebrated*
Adar 15	*feasted*	*rested & celebrated*

🔸 The point of sorting out who did what on which day is to explain why the victory celebrations were held on different days in different regions of Persia. As the story draws near to the end, we are once again where we were at the beginning—a big feast. What characterizes the celebration here in chapter 9?

celebrated, feasted, gave gifts of food
feasting & gladness
gave gifts to the poor

Chronology in Esther
The events of Esther unfold over a period of 10 years.[6]

Reference	Event	Month	Day	Year of Ahasuerus's Reign	Year
1:3	Ahasuerus holds his banquets.			3	483 BC
2:16	Esther goes to Ahasuerus.	10		7	479 BC
3:7	Haman casts his lots.	1		12	474 BC
3:12	Haman issues his decree.	1	13	12	474 BC
3:13	Date planned for annihilation of the Jews.	12	13	13	473 BC
8:9	Mordecai issues his decree.	3	23	13	473 BC
8:12; 9:1	Day upon which Jews could defend themselves from attack.	12	13	13	473 BC
9:6-10, 20-22	Ten sons of Haman executed; Feast of Purim celebrated.	12	14, 15	13	473 BC

LET'S TALK

1. One of the big takeaways from the book of Esther is that God fulfills his promises through ordinary providences in everyday life. In fact, he works this way much more often than through miraculous means. Given that this is true, it means that God is working out his purposes in every detail of our very own lives. Nothing is wasted; no circumstance is meaningless. The truth is, everything going on in our lives today is somehow, some way preparatory for what God has planned for tomorrow. How has our study of Esther up to this point changed or refined your view of God and your present circumstances? Can you identify a circumstance from your past that has since played a significant role in your life?

A FEAST FOR ALL TIME

ESTHER 9:20-10:3

One of the primary purposes of the book of Esther is to explain how the annual Jewish Feast of Purim originated, and that's where we are now in the story. This annual feast got its start with the grand victory celebration of God's people when their enemies were conquered in Persia. Rural Jews feasted on Adar 14, while the Jews living in Susa held a feast on Adar 15. And what began as a one-time celebration of joy and rest became an annual tradition that is still celebrated by Jewish people today.

1. A CALL TO CELEBRATE (9:20-23)

Mordecai records plans for the feast and distributes throughout the provinces of Persia instructions for how it's to be celebrated.

✦ Both Adar 14 and Adar 15, the original days of celebration, were to become a national Jewish holiday spread over those same two days every year. According to Mordecai's instructions, what particular reversals were to be commemorated each year?

sorrow was turned to gladness
mourning was turned to joy

What activities were to occur during the annual celebration?

feast, celebrate, give gifts to each other of food and presents to the poor.

2. THE LOT WAS CAST (9:24-28)

All the Jews in Persia were happy to obligate themselves each year to commemorate the downfall of Israel's ancient enemy, the Amalekites, represented by Haman.

What reminder is provided here in this passage about how Haman had determined the day for attacking the Jews?

he had plotted to crush & destroy the Jews by casting lots (Purim) (the date was determined by the casting of lots.

We know that Haman's evil plot failed, and in verse 25 we are reminded that circumstances changed so that Haman's evil plan "should return on his own head." What does Psalm 7:12–16 add to our understanding of this wording here in verse 25 and of God's role in Haman's tragic end?

"They dig a deep pit to trap others but fall into it themselves. The trouble they wish on others backfires on them. The violence & the plan falls on their own heads

In the ESV Bible, the translation we are using for this study, verse 26 begins with the word "Therefore." In fact, the verse contains two *therefores*. Whenever we encounter this word, it indicates that what is about to come is linked to what went before. Maybe you've heard Bible study teachers say, "We need to ask what the 'therefore' is *there for.*"

So that is the question here. What do the *therefores* in verse 26 tell us? The same question applies for whichever Bible translation you are using, where some of you have "so that" or "because of" or "that is why": what *reason* or *condition* is being revealed?

it is called "Purim" "casting lots" for the date that was selected by casting lots

It's hard to think of God's people establishing a joyful feast to commemorate the death and destruction of anyone, even long-feared enemies. How does Psalm 16:5–6 help explain the joy associated with this occasion?

The LORD guards and protects all that is ours from Him.

What commitment do the Jews make concerning the Feast of Purim?

" agreed to unnaugurate this commitment and to pass it on to their descendents and to all who became Jews. They declared they would never fail to celebrate the two days of Purim

3. THE IMPORTANCE OF PURIM (9:29-32)

Esther reenters the picture here, where she and Mordecai together confirm the continuation of this important feast. The fact that there is a second letter (v. 29) likely means that extra effort was needed to unify the urban Jews and the rural Jews in celebrating Purim on the same day each year. If you have ever planned a wedding reception or another major celebration, you know how complicated the details can be. And the larger the gathering, the harder it is. So we can understand why authoritative letters were needed to get Purim on the right track.

✦ This is the last we hear of Esther. What do you observe about Esther's position in Persia at this point? What words clue you in?

a position of authority

"wrote with full power & authority"
"the command of Esther confirmed these practices"

Esthers decree confirmed

✦ All God's people in Persia obligated themselves to keep this joyful feast each year, just as they kept more somber occasions that involved not joy but fasting and lament (see, for example, Leviticus 16:29–31). This final section of Esther 9 (vv. 29–32) begins and ends with the same action. What is it, and why do you think this is recorded for us?

wrote a law confirming the festival

Purim Today

Jewish people continue to celebrate Purim with a joyful spirit. Participants often dress up in costumes to celebrate. The night before the celebrating begins, they attend synagogue, where the story of Esther is read. Children delight in this tradition, because they are given rattles to shake whenever Haman's name is read. They hold seriously the obligations established by Mordecai and Esther, marking the occasion with feasting and sending food gifts. They also give to the poor at Purim.

4. THE GREATNESS OF MORDECAI (10:1-3)

King Ahasuerus continues to govern his vast empire, reinstating the taxes he had stopped temporarily during Esther's inauguration as his new queen (see Esther 2:18). Directly underneath the king is Mordecai. He has risen to tremendous power in Persia.

✤ Why was Mordecai a popular leader?

Because he continued to work for the good of his people and to speak up for the welfare of their descendents"

He had moral integrity + character

The ending of the book of Esther isn't a random tying up of loose ends. To the contrary, it's hugely significant. The greatness of Mordecai actually points to, or foreshadows, someone so much greater than Mordecai himself. Mordecai points to Jesus, who came to earth to speak peace to his people and seek their welfare. That's why this seemingly anticlimactic ending to our story is actually the most exciting part.

During the course of studying Esther, we've seen how the book is connected to earlier Bible history. We noted that the Jews were living in Persia due to the faithlessness of earlier generations. Due to sin, God had sent his people into exile, out of their home in the promised land. But along with the exile had come God's promise of hope for redemption and rescue, which continues to unfold in the events of Esther with the downfall of Haman and his wicked plot. That too had been promised centuries earlier, in God's decree to wipe out the Amalekites (Exodus 17:14–15). But the story of Esther points not only to the past but also to the future. And most of all, the story of Esther shows us the amazing power and providence of our great God.

✤ How do the passages below enhance or fulfill the big-picture Bible themes we've studied in Esther as well as what we have learned about the character of God? Some of the themes to look for include God's faithfulness and providence, his justice, and his power to deliver his people. It's also really fun to uncover his powerful reversals.

• captives will be released
- blind will see
- oppressed will be set free
· Luke 4:16–19

God's plans & purposes) have been
fulfilled in Jesus Christ
V. 21

· John 10:27–30

Everyone of the sheep, chosen by the
Good Shepherd are secure forever

· Romans 8:28–30

God knew us and chose us in Jesus
before the foundation of the world "before" in the
beginning" All of the daily circumstances of
our life led us to the day we repented &
believed.
· Ephesians 1:11–12
" And this is the plan: "at the right time"
trust in His promises) He chose us in
advance and makes everything work out accordy
to His plan, every mundane detail of every day
· Colossians 1:16–20

Christ existed before all things
and God's plan through Him was
established before all things

· Revelation 19:6–9

We look forward to the culmination
of our salvation. The wedding feast.

LET'S TALK

1. Who would you say is the hero or heroine of the story and why?

2. The Feast of Purim primarily celebrates not so much the *death* of God's enemies as the *rest* or *relief* that their death provided God's people. How is this a picture of the rest given to us in Christ? How have you personally experienced Jesus's words in Matthew 11:28–30?

The burden of being perfect and keeping
my right standing w/ God through obedience.

....

....

....

3. As we end our study of Esther, summarize what you have learned about—

· the big story of the whole Bible:

....

....

....

....

....

....

....

....

....

· the character of Almighty God:

....

....

....

....

....

....

· salvation in Jesus Christ:

HELPFUL RESOURCES
ON ESTHER

Ash, Christopher. *Teaching Ruth and Esther: From Text to Message*. Edited by David Jackman and Jon Gemmell. Scotland: Christian Focus, 2018.

Cosper, Mike. *Faith among the Faithless: Learning from Esther How to Live in a World Gone Mad*. Nashville, TN: Nelson, 2018.

ESV Study Bible. Wheaton, IL: Crossway, 2008.

Fox, Michael V. *Character and Ideology in the Book of Esther*. 2nd ed. Grand Rapids, MI: Eerdmans, 2001.

Hazony, Yoram. *God and Politics in Esther*. New York: Cambridge University Press, 2016.

Jobes, Karen H. *Esther*. NIV Application Commentary. Grand Rapids, MI: Zondervan Academic, 2011.

Nielson, Kathleen. *Ruth and Esther: A 12-Week Study*. Knowing the Bible. Edited by J. I. Packer and Dane C. Ortlund. Wheaton, IL: Crossway, 2014.

NOTES

1. "The Persian Empire at the Time of Esther" map is taken from page 850 of the ESV® Study Bible (The Holy Bible, English Standard Version®), copyright © 2008 by Crossway. Used by permission. All rights reserved.
2. A. Shapur Shahbazi, "Harem i. in Ancient Iran," *Encyclopaedia Iranica*, last modified March 6, 2012, accessed June 4, 2019, http://www.iranicaonline.org/articles/harem-i.
3. Karen Jobes, *Esther*, NIV Application Commentary (Grand Rapids, MI: Zondervan Academic, 2011), 146.
4. Yoram Hazony, *God and Politics in Esther* (New York: Cambridge University Press, 2016), 133.
5. Jobes, *Esther*, 188.
6. "Chronology in Esther" chart, taken from page 855 of the ESV® Study Bible.

Forthcoming Volumes
in This Series

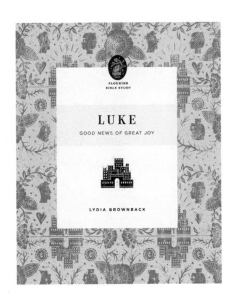

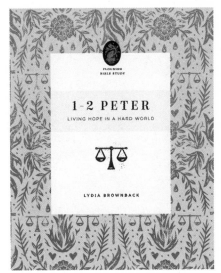

For more information, visit **crossway.org**.